IMMIGRANTS
WHO LED THE WAY

BY DANIELLE SMITH-LLERA

CAPSTONE PRESS
a capstone imprint

Capstone Captivate is published by Capstone Press, an imprint of Capstone.
1710 Roe Crest Drive
North Mankato, Minnesota 56003
www.capstonepub.com

Library of Congress Cataloging-in-Publication Data
Names: Smith-Llera, Danielle, 1971– author.
Title: Immigrants who led the way / Danielle Smith-Llera.
Description: North Mankato, Minnesota : Capstone Press, [2021] | Includes bibliographical references and index. | Audience: Ages: 8–11 | Audience: Grades: 4–6 | Summary: "Some of the most important American products and ideas have been developed by people born outside the United States. They have influenced every part of U.S. culture, from what people wear and drive to how they stay healthy, how they communicate with each other, and what they do for fun. Meet 25 immigrants who have led the way with life-saving inventions, by opening up sports to women and people of color, and so much more"—Provided by publisher.
Identifiers: LCCN 2020034848 (print) | LCCN 2020034849 (ebook) | ISBN 9781496695949 (hardcover) | ISBN 9781496696786 (paperback) | ISBN 9781977154439 (pdf) | ISBN 9781977156105 (kindle edition)
Subjects: LCSH: Immigrants—United States—Biography—Juvenile literature. | Successful people—United States—Biography—Juvenile literature. | Inventors—United States—Biography—Juvenile literature.
Classification: LCC E184.A1 S663 2021 (print) | LCC E184.A1 (ebook) | DDC 305.9/0691200922 [B]—dc23
LC record available at https://lccn.loc.gov/2020034848
LC ebook record available at https://lccn.loc.gov/2020034849

Image Credits
Getty Images: Bettmann, 23, 36, Carl Court, 55, Denver Post, 39, Gado/University of New Hampshire, 52, Mondadori Portfolio/Archivio Apg, 34, Sygma/Brooks Kraft LLC, 41, The LIFE Images Collection/Terry Ashe, 27; Library of Congress: 5 (top left, bottom right), 7, 33, 47, 49; NASA: Joel Kowsky, 31; The New York Public Library: 5 (middle right), 51; Newscom: Album/Documenta, 5 (top right), 8, picture-alliance/dpa/Jens Wolf, 12, Reuters/Daniel Becerril, 59, Reuters/Michael Crabtree, 25, Reuters/Robert Galbraith, 17, SportsChrome/Sport The Library, 29, Universal Images Group, 21, Xinhua News Agency/Wang Ping, 5 (bottom left), 58, ZUMA Press/Paul Bersebach, 43, ZUMA Press/Ryan Garza, 45; Shutterstock: aijaphoto, 20, armmit, 10, Bangkok Click Studio, cover, 1, 5 (back), mark reinstein, 5 (middle left), 57, My Hardy (background texture), 13, 27, 42, 49, 59, Narin C, 42, Puwadol Jaturawutthichai, 37 (flags), Richard Cavalleri, 14; U.S. Patent and Trademark Office: 19

Editorial Credits
Editor: Michelle Bisson; Designer: Kayla Rossow and Tracy Davies; Media Researcher: Svetlana Zhurkin; Production Specialist: Tori Abraham

All internet sites appearing in back matter were available and accurate when this book was sent to press.

TABLE OF CONTENTS

INTRODUCTION

Many famous American products and ideas have been developed by people born outside the United States. These immigrants have influenced every part of U.S. culture. They have changed what people wear and drive. They have changed how people communicate with each other. They have changed how people stay healthy and what they do for fun.

The U.S. has attracted creative and determined people. These people have left their home countries for many different reasons. Some have fled prejudice, war, or unfair governments. Others simply want freedom to choose their professions. They have come to the United States to complete their training. They often stay to apply their knowledge and skills to helping others. They have improved the lives of people across the nation and around the world.

Hedy Lamarr

Nikola Tesla

Claude McKay

Isabel Allende

Yo-Yo Ma

Albert Einstein

CHAPTER ONE

IMPROVING LIVES

U.S. immigrants have created a great number of life-changing inventions. Immigrants' ideas and hard work have improved lives across the nation and the globe. Their inventions keep people safe, comfortable, entertained, and informed.

NIKOLA TESLA

(1856–1943)
Born in Smiljan, Croatia

As a child, Nikola Tesla noticed that petting his cat made sparks. He wondered why. Tesla studied electrical engineering in college. At age 24, he thought of a new way to create electricity. At the time, electrical power systems flowed in one direction—the way power travels from a battery to a device. This is DC, or direct current, power. Tesla discovered that electricity switching directions—up to 60 times per second—creates more power. It also travels greater distances. This is AC, or alternating current, power.

Tesla moved to New York City in 1884. He worked for Thomas Edison, the inventor of the first practical and inexpensive lightbulb. Edison did not accept that AC power was more useful than DC power. So Tesla quit working for him.

Nikola Tesla has become more famous in the 21st century than he was in his lifetime. Only now do people really understand the importance of his inventions.

Tesla patented an AC motor design in 1887. George Westinghouse, a wealthy entrepreneur and engineer, introduced Tesla's invention to the world. Millions of visitors to the 1893 Chicago World's Fair saw a display of 100,000 lamps. Tesla's motor design created the electricity.

Today, refrigerators, power tools, automobiles, and most electric motors in the world use Tesla's invention. In 1891, he designed new technology for electricity to travel without wires. Today it is used in radios, TVs, smartphones, remote controls, chargers, and other wireless electronics.

HEDY LAMARR

(1914–2000)
Born in Vienna, Austria

When Hedy Lamarr arrived in California in 1937, she got right to work. For two decades, she played stylish characters in Hollywood movies. Her face inspired Disney's Snow White character. But Lamarr believed people's minds were more interesting than their looks.

Hedy Lamarr was famous as an actor in her time, but also is known today for her work as an inventor.

Lamarr grew up curious about machines. At 5 years old, Lamarr took apart a music box to understand how it worked. As an actor, she kept an inventor's table in the trailer where she took breaks. She once invented a new design for airplane wings. It was inspired by the shape of bird wings and fish fins.

In 1940, Lamarr felt guilty about her easy life in Hollywood. Many people were suffering through World War II (1939–1945). She thought of an idea that could defeat Nazi Germany. Allied ships used radio signals to guide torpedoes. Deadly German submarines were their targets. But the Germans hacked these signals. The torpedoes too often missed. Lamarr found a way to make messages too complex for enemies to understand. These radio signals switched quickly between frequencies. Her partner, George Antheil, was a composer and inventor. He built the model. They patented the "Secret Communications System" in 1942. The military did not use the invention for two decades. Yet her invention is used in today's cell phones, Wi-Fi, Bluetooth, and the Global Positioning System (GPS).

DID YOU KNOW?

About 30 percent of U.S. inventors today were born in another country, according to a 2017 study.

GIULIANA TESORO

(1921–2002)
Born in Venice, Italy

In the 1930s, Giuliana Tesoro and other Jewish people in Italy could not attend university. The fascist government considered them enemies. Tesoro moved to the U.S. in 1939. She completed her PhD in organic chemistry. As a chemist, Tesoro held more than 125 patents in her lifetime. These chemical inventions saved lives.

Giuliana Tesoro's work has been invaluable to the military, among other organizations and industries.

In the mid-1900s, female chemists struggled to find challenging research work. Male scientists usually got those jobs. Tesoro's first job in a lab was writing about chemistry. But she wanted to do more.

For more than 50 years, Tesoro was a researcher. She became an expert on synthetic fibers. Polyester, rayon, nylon, and other plastics were sturdy and flexible. By the 1970s, they were taking the place of cotton, wool, and other natural fibers. Unfortunately, these synthetic materials easily caught fire. And they were everywhere. They were in clothing, carpets, airplane seats, electronics, and more.

Tesoro created new chemical mixtures to add to textiles and other materials. These mixtures slowed or stopped the spread of fire. She invented a new flame-retardant fiber too. Today, these chemicals and materials are used by the military and by the aerospace, automotive, transportation, and construction industries.

RALPH BAER

(1922–2014)
Born in Rodalben, Germany

In 2009, Ralph Baer showed the prototype of the first game console that he had invented in the 1960s.

Jewish children could not attend school under Germany's Nazi government. Ralph Baer was Jewish. In 1938, when he was 16, he and his family moved to the U.S. He trained as a TV engineer. He received more than 150 patents in his lifetime. One was for the popular electronic memory game *Simon*.

Computer programmers created the first interactive electronic game in the early 1960s. But computers were far too expensive for use at home.

One day in 1966, while waiting for a bus, Baer had an idea. Millions of people in the U.S. owned TV sets. What if people used them to play games? But how could he design games that could be played on TVs?

Baer had a special workshop at an engineering company. He worked with a small team. They worked on prototypes for years. Finally, Baer took his invention to the U.S. Patent Office. Players used controls to bounce a dot around on the screen, playing a version of tennis. In 1972, the first home video gaming system, the Magnavox Odyssey, became available for sale. Today, the gaming industry makes billions of dollars a year.

INVENTOR'S WORKSHOP

Anyone can see Ralph Baer's inventor's workshop. He was 84 years old when he donated it to the National Museum of American History in Washington, D.C. The museum is part of the Smithsonian Institution. The workshop was set up in the area for U.S. innovations. Baer's soldering gun and drawers of electronic parts are on display. Visitors can also view Baer's video game test units, models, notes, and sketches.

FAZLUR RAHMAN KHAN

(1929–1982)
Born in Dhaka, Bangladesh

New York City's Empire State Building was completed in 1931. For 40 years, many engineers believed it was the tallest building possible. A taller building would be too heavy to stand safely, many thought. Fazlur Rahman Khan proved them wrong.

The Willis Tower was the world's tallest building for more than two decades.

In 1952, Khan moved to Chicago. He earned his PhD in structural engineering and then began working on buildings. It was a challenge to construct skyscrapers in Chicago. The winds are strong. The ground is swampy. Khan wondered what it would feel like to be a skyscraper there. It helped inspire his ideas.

A skyscraper usually needed a heavy frame inside for support. Khan invented a "tubular system." It gave a skyscraper a strong frame on the outside. Khan's invention made buildings lighter. It also allowed them to be taller and cheaper to build.

In 1972, the World Trade Center in New York City was completed. Its architects used Khan's structural design to create the Twin Towers. The taller tower rose to 1,368 feet (417 meters)—more than 100 feet (30 m) higher than the Empire State Building. A year later, Khan helped set a new record. Chicago's Willis Tower—first named the Sears Tower—used bundles of tube structures to rise to 1,450 feet (442 m). It remained the world's tallest building for almost 25 years. Some of the world's tallest buildings today use Khan's system.

SERGEY BRIN

(1973–)
Born in Moscow, Russia

Sergey Brin is grateful his family left Russia, then part of the Soviet Union, in 1979. The Russian government stopped his father from studying astronomy because he was Jewish. Brin grew up in Maryland, where he was free to choose his career. He used his talent for math to make the internet more useful.

In 1996, Brin and another computer science graduate student, Larry Page, began working on an exciting project. The two designed a new internet search engine. These internet tools collect lists of websites. At the time, search engines simply used keywords typed by users. People had to figure out which sites were most useful. Many did not have the information users needed. So Brin designed a mathematical algorithm. This is a set of instructions for computers to follow. Brin's algorithm finds websites with the most links to other websites. These sites are likely to be the most popular. So, they appear first in an internet search.

Sergey Brin revolutionized the way people search the internet when he and Larry Page created Google.

Brin and Page introduced Google to the public in 1997. The project began in a university dorm room. By 2020, it had grown into a business worth $1 trillion. Every day, the amount of information on the internet grows. Google helps people find what they need there.

CHAPTER TWO

GUIDING OTHERS

Strong leaders can inspire others with their ideas. They can also organize people to turn their ideas into reality. In the U.S., many of these leaders have been immigrants.

LEVI STRAUSS

(1829–1902)
Born in Buttenheim, Germany

Levi Strauss always had a talent for business. As a teenager, he walked around New York City selling sewing supplies, kettles, and other goods. In 1853, Strauss left for California, like many other people looking for new opportunities. He started a company called Levi Strauss & Co. It supplied shops with fabric, clothing, and other goods. He soon had many customers across the Pacific region, and even in Hawaii and Japan.

This drawing was submitted to get a patent for Davis's jeans. It shows how the rivets made the pockets and pants seams stronger.

In 1872, a tailor asked Strauss to help him sell a new product. Jacob Davis was an immigrant from Latvia. He made work pants out of blue cotton. He hammered metal fasteners, or rivets, into the seams to make them sturdy. In 1873, Strauss and Davis applied for a patent for work pants with rivets. They would become known as "jeans."

Strauss knew how to make Levi's jeans popular. His salespeople handed out colorful brochures. He had advertisements painted on buildings. He added the Levi's logo in 1886. It showed two horses tugging on a pair of the tough pants. It was easy to recognize.

Today, people all over the world spend billions of dollars on jeans each year. Levi's clothing can be sporty or fashionable. It reminds many people of freedom and adventure. These are some of the reasons why people first moved to the American West.

DID YOU KNOW?

Jeans for women were revolutionary when Levi's introduced them.

For more than 60 years, Levi's only sold men's jeans. The company introduced the first jeans designed for women in 1934. It was a bold fashion statement. Most women wore only skirts or dresses at the time. They started wearing pants in the mid-1940s.

JAMES NAISMITH

(1861–1939)
Born in Almonte, Canada

In the winter of 1891, James Naismith was coaching college students in Massachusetts. Cold weather trapped them inside the gymnasium with little to do. Naismith had moved to the U.S. a year earlier to study and teach physical education. He needed to find a competitive game that could be played safely indoors. That winter, Naismith invented basketball.

James Naismith invented basketball as an indoor winter sport.

Naismith borrowed from many outdoor games. English rugby inspired basketball's jump shot. Basketball players pass the ball like American rugby players do. As with lacrosse goals, basketball hoops stand on either side of the court. Players must aim carefully at raised baskets. The game "Duck-on-a-Rock" inspired this. It was a rock-throwing game Naismith played as a child in Canada.

Naismith's students played their first games with a soccer ball. They aimed for peach baskets nailed to balconies in the gym. Players soon helped develop Naismith's game further. For example, they began dribbling to move the ball around the court.

Many of Naismith's students introduced others to basketball. Colleges were playing each other's teams by the end of the 1800s. Naismith presented basketball medals in the 1936 Olympics in Berlin. Today, basketball is a unique symbol of U.S. culture around the world. Millions play the game. Loyal fans cheer them on.

LIZ CLAIBORNE

(1929–2007)
Born in Brussels, Belgium

Liz Claiborne moved to New York after winning a fashion contest at age 20.

As a teenager, Liz Claiborne sketched a coat that won a fashion contest. It changed her life. In 1949, she moved to New York City. There she began a career in the fashion industry. For 40 years, she worked as a clothing designer. In 1976, Claiborne and her partners started a new fashion business. They named it after her. It made large profits, even in its first year.

The women's rights movement was inspiring women to pursue new careers. Since World War II, the number of women working outside their homes had tripled. Claiborne believed women needed new fashions for new jobs.

Claiborne's designs were inspired by studying art in Europe. But she also introduced a new idea. She believed women should choose their style for the workplace. Claiborne sold separate pieces of clothing in many colors and styles. Customers could mix and match them. Claiborne's clothing was practical and creative. It was also less expensive than other designer clothing.

In 1986, Liz Claiborne joined *Fortune* magazine's list of most successful businesses in the U.S. It was the first company founded by a woman to make the list. It was also the first company with a female chief executive officer.

MADELEINE ALBRIGHT

(1937–)
Born in Prague, the Czech Republic

Madeleine Albright's family fled the present-day Czech Republic in 1949. A new, strict, communist government had taken over. It was dangerous for anyone who supported democracy. The Albrights arrived in the U.S. as refugees.

As secretary of state, Madeleine Albright had many different missions. One of her toughest was trying to make peace in the Middle East.

Albright studied law and government. She taught in a university as a professor of international relations. This is the study of how countries and international organizations work together. In 1993, President Bill Clinton chose her as ambassador to the United Nations. This is a council of world representatives. It works to keep peaceful relationships between countries. The members also work to help victims of poverty, war, natural disasters, and other challenges.

In 1996, Clinton gave Albright the nation's top job in international relations. She served as his secretary of state. She was the first woman to serve in this important role. For four years, she invited nations to join the North Atlantic Treaty Organization (NATO). The NATO nations agree to protect each other with their militaries. Secretary of State Albright also fought for human rights. She supported military attacks on the Serbian government in 1999. It was murdering its Muslim citizens. Albright also worked to limit nuclear weapons. And she persuaded more countries to fight climate change.

PINS WITH ATTITUDE

As ambassador to the United Nations, Madeleine Albright communicated her opinions to world leaders in a special way. Once, Iraqi newspapers had called her a serpent. So she fastened a snake pin to her jacket before a meeting with Iraqi leaders. TV cameras zoomed in on the pin. She knew the pin was showing her tough attitude. Albright wore flowers and balloon pins to other meetings. This meant she felt positive about them. She also wore turtle or crab pins. This meant her meetings might be slow and difficult. Sometimes, she needed to be extra tough. Then, she wore her wasp pin.

Madeleine Albright's snake pin was more than a fashion statement.

NADIA COMANECI

(1961–)
Born in Onesti, Romania

Nadia Comaneci arrived by plane in New York City on December 1, 1989. Romania's leader, Nicolae Ceausescu, punished and killed people who criticized his government. The U.S. gave Comaneci asylum. She would be in great danger if she returned to Romania. The U.S. welcomed the 28-year-old gymnast. She was a celebrity.

Comaneci began studying gymnastics at age 6. By age 13, she had won European competitions with perfect scores.

In 1976, 14-year-old Comaneci competed in the Olympics in Montreal, Canada. Her first event was the uneven bars. The judges could not find a single mistake in her routine. She earned the first perfect score in Olympics gymnastic history. No one had received a perfect 10.00 in an Olympic gymnastics event. The scoreboards were designed to display scores up to 9.99, not 10.00. The scoreboard displayed her score as a 1.00. Comaneci won a total of seven perfect scores at that Olympic competition.

Nadia Comaneci made history at the 1976 Olympics.

Comaneci won 21 gold medals at international competitions. Yet she is most famous for the first perfect score at the Olympics. It inspired athletes around the world to attempt what seemed impossible. Comaneci now teaches and coaches young gymnasts in Oklahoma.

ELON MUSK

(1971–)
Born in Pretoria, South Africa

At age 12, Elon Musk taught himself computer coding. He created a simple video game and sold it to a computer magazine for $500. Today, the entrepreneur's ideas have made billions of dollars. They have also helped improve human life.

Musk had always dreamed of living in the U.S. By 2002, he was a multimillionaire—in California. He had founded and sold PayPal. This is a company that manages online payments. Then he founded SpaceX. The company designs and launches spacecraft. It was the first private company to deliver supplies to the International Space Station. In 2018, SpaceX successfully launched a rocket twice as powerful as any ever built. In 2020, a SpaceX spacecraft carrying two NASA astronauts docked at the International Space Station. It was the first time a private company had flown astronauts into orbit. Musk hopes SpaceX will one day take passengers on trips to Mars.

Musk hopes to improve how people travel on Earth too. In 2003, he founded Tesla Motors. He

Until recently, Elon Musk (left) was best known for his electric car. But the successful launches of SpaceX have expanded his reach—literally—into space.

wants to prove that electric cars can be faster than gasoline-powered cars. Musk also founded a company that designs technology to dig tunnels. He hopes that passengers can ride pods through them. He believes they can travel at more than 600 miles (965 kilometers) per hour.

Musk wants to learn more about the human brain too. In 2017, he founded Neuralink. This company designs technology to implant inside the body. It helps the brain share information with computers.

CHAPTER THREE

UNCOVERING MYSTERIES

Many scientists have immigrated to the U.S. Some have made great discoveries. They have improved the health of people's bodies and minds. They have also helped explain great mysteries about how the universe works.

ALBERT EINSTEIN

(1879–1955)
Born in Ulm, Germany

Albert Einstein arrived in the U.S. as a refugee in 1933. This was the year Adolf Hitler rose to power in Germany. The Nazis raided Einstein's office and burned his books. Einstein was Jewish. He lost his job as a university physics professor in Berlin. But Einstein had already changed people's understanding of the world.

For thousands of years, people wondered if matter was made of tiny parts. These parts are called atoms. In 1905, Einstein used math to prove atoms exist.

He also discovered something new about light. Scientists believed that light was made of waves. Einstein said that light could also be made of tiny particles.

In 1940, Albert Einstein (left) received his certificate of U.S. citizenship from a judge.

In 1915, Einstein changed the world of physics. That year, Einstein explained how massive objects affect space. He claimed that they can even bend time. During a 1919 solar eclipse, scientists saw the sun bending starlight. This was proof of Einstein's general theory of relativity.

More discoveries have proved that Einstein's theory is correct. In 2016, scientists used special equipment to pick up vibrations from space. They resulted from a collision of two massive objects in space. These vibrations prove that space and time can change shape. Einstein's theory also made scientists imagine black holes. In 2019, the world saw the first photograph of a black hole. Einstein was right again.

RITA LEVI-MONTALCINI

(1909–2012)
Born in Turin, Italy

Rita Levi-Montalcini had a laboratory in her
bedroom in Italy. In the United States, she worked at
Washington University in St. Louis, Missouri.

Rita Levi-Montalcini moved to St. Louis, Missouri, in 1947. The neurobiologist was invited to research nerve cells. They carry important messages between parts of the body. They tell muscles to move and allow eyes to see.

Levi-Montalcini was born in Italy. But she did not have the same rights as other Italians. Fascist prime minister Benito Mussolini believed that Jewish people were enemies. Levi-Montalcini was Jewish. She was not allowed to work at a university lab. So she set up a laboratory in her bedroom and made her own lab tools. There she began the research that led her to the U.S.

Levi-Montalcini studied chicken embryos, or unhatched chicks. She wondered how many different kinds of nerve cells exist to do so many different jobs. Levi-Montalcini believed a chemical in the body made it happen. In the late 1940s, Levi-Montalcini and biochemist Stanley Cohen discovered this chemical was a form of protein. They shared the 1986 Nobel Prize in Medicine for the discovery. Levi-Montalcini's work has helped today's medical researchers. These researchers study how to treat wounds, tumors, and conditions such as Alzheimer's disease.

SUBRAHMANYAN CHANDRASEKHAR

(1910–1995)
Born in Lahore, Pakistan

Subrahmanyan Chandrasekhar's theory of black holes expanded our view of the universe.

Physicist Subrahmanyan Chandrasekhar left England in 1937, disappointed. Other scientists said his new theory about stars was impossible. But he was sure his math was correct. Chandrasekhar moved to the U.S. to teach and do research at the University of Chicago. There, he would find scientists who supported his ideas.

What happens once stars run out of energy? Chandrasekhar had a theory. Scientists knew that most of a star's matter crushes into a tiny object. This object is one-millionth the size of the original star.

That's as if a car was crushed down into the size of an olive. But scientists wondered why the star's matter didn't collapse even more. Chandrasekhar turned to Albert Einstein's theory of relativity. It explains the behavior of massive objects like stars. Chandrasekhar used math to discover that a dying star can behave strangely. It can crush down smaller and smaller, forever. These strange objects were later called "black holes."

Chandrasekhar's theory changed astrophysics. In 1983, he won the Nobel Prize in Physics. This was 53 years after he first made his discovery. Today scientists still use Chandrasekhar's math to understand black holes.

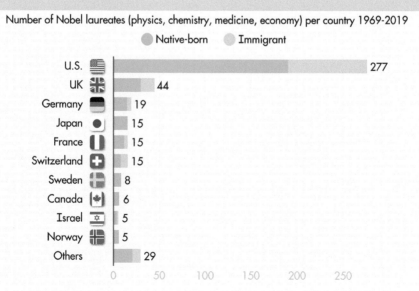

IMMIGRANTS' SHARE OF NOBEL PRIZES IN SCIENCES

Number of Nobel laureates (physics, chemistry, medicine, economy) per country 1969-2019

● Native-born   ● Immigrant

U.S.	277
UK	44
Germany	19
Japan	15
France	15
Switzerland	15
Sweden	8
Canada	6
Israel	5
Norway	5
Others	29

0   50   100   150   200   250

ELISABETH KÜBLER-ROSS

(1926–2004)
Born in Zurich, Switzerland

In middle school, Elisabeth Kübler-Ross knew she wanted to become a doctor. In 1958, she moved to New York to study psychiatry. This branch of medicine studies the mind. Kübler-Ross created a new branch of medicine. Its goal is to care for people at the end of their lives.

In the mid-1960s, Kübler-Ross was working in a hospital. She noticed a group of patients who needed help. There was no cure for their conditions. At the time, doctors avoided talking about death. As a psychiatrist, Kübler-Ross noticed dying people were lonely and afraid. She wanted to help them.

Kübler-Ross interviewed thousands of patients and medical professionals. She discovered a pattern. Patients often felt "five stages of grief." They include anger, sadness, and acceptance. In 1969, Kübler-Ross published this theory in her book *On Death and Dying*. Medical professionals and patients' families have read and learned from this book ever since.

Elisabeth Kübler-Ross spoke about the "five stages of grief" for decades after she first developed the theory and wrote a book about it.

In the 1970s, Kübler-Ross's work inspired medical professionals, counselors, and families to work together. They cared for the bodies and emotions of dying people. This is called hospice care. By the 1980s, medical schools made sure future doctors studied thanatology. This is the study of death and dying.

MARIO MOLINA

(1943–)
Born in Mexico City, Mexico

In the 1960s, activists across the U.S. spoke up against pollution. They inspired a chemist named Mario Molina. He had moved to California in 1968 to study physical chemistry. This is the study of how atoms and molecules fit together. Molina made a discovery that helped protect life on Earth from dangerous pollution.

In a California research lab, Molina studied human-made chemicals called chlorofluorocarbons (CFCs). These compounds were used in aerosol spray cans, inside refrigerators, and in making plastic foams. In 1973, Molina used a computer model to study how CFCs behave. They float high above Earth and destroy ozone molecules. Ozone shields Earth from much of the sun's ultraviolet radiation. This dangerous light damages cells and causes cancer.

For a decade, scientists, politicians, and business leaders ignored Molina's findings. But in 1983, British scientist Joseph Farman discovered a hole in the ozone. It was above Antarctica. It was about the

In 1995, Mario Molina won the Nobel Prize in Chemistry for his ozone hole research.

size of the U.S. Soon after, U.S. atmospheric chemist Susan Solomon studied the hole too. She proved Molina's theory was correct. In 1987, world leaders finally began work to reduce the use of CFCs. Molina and his lab director, Sherwood Rowland, shared the 1995 Nobel Prize in Chemistry.

A THEORY ABOUT OZONE HOLES

Susan Solomon braved Antarctica's harsh winter. She was there to test Mario Molina's theory about ozone holes. She believed icy crystals in the clouds were the problem. Dangerous chemical reactions took place on their flat surfaces.

Solomon and her team worked in almost 24-hour darkness. But Solomon didn't need sunlight. She was looking for high levels of chlorine monoxide (ClO). That chemical would prove that ultraviolet light was breaking apart CFCs. When CFCs break apart, they release chlorine (Cl) molecules. A Cl molecule steals oxygen from an ozone molecule (O_3) to create O_2 and ClO. Solomon did find high levels of ClO molecules. She knew Molina's computer models were correct.

This diagram shows what happens when the ozone layer becomes depleted.

DAVID HO

(1952–)
Born in Taichung City, Taiwan

David Ho was 12 when he moved to California in 1965. At first, he struggled to learn English and fit in at his new school. He never imagined that one day a Los Angeles Lakers basketball star would ask him for help. In 1991, Earvin "Magic" Johnson announced that he was infected with human immunodeficiency virus (HIV). Ho was a world expert on this dangerous disease. He discovered a treatment. It changed the lives of Johnson and millions of other HIV patients.

Magic Johnson (left) listens as Dr. David Ho talks about the creation of Johnson's foundation to help combat AIDS.

Ho was working in a hospital in 1981. He was surprised to see new patients with weakened immune systems. This is the system that defends the body from disease. These patients had the first known cases of HIV. There was no helpful treatment in the 1980s. HIV develops into acquired immunodeficiency syndrome (AIDS). People with AIDS cannot fight diseases and infections like healthy people can. For example, people with AIDS die of pneumonia at much higher rates than others.

Ho used computer models to study how HIV/AIDS takes over the body. The virus takes over cells. The virus spreads as the infected cells multiply. By 1996, Ho had developed a combination of drugs called antiretroviral therapy treatment (ART). ART slowed, or even stopped, the progress of HIV/AIDS. People with HIV could now live longer, healthier lives.

MONA HANNA-ATTISHA

(1976–)
Born in Sheffield, United Kingdom

Mona Hanna-Attisha's parents fled a dangerous government in Iraq. They arrived in England before she was born. She moved to Michigan as a 4-year-old. She is a pediatrician and activist who helps thousands of U.S. children have a better future too.

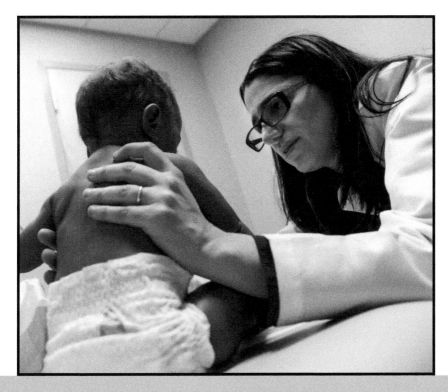

Dr. Mona Hanna-Attisha has always focused her medical practice and activism on the goal of helping children.

In 2015, Hanna-Attisha was working at a hospital in Flint, Michigan. A water expert told her the city's drinking water was dangerous. For 18 months, that water had come from the Flint River. It contained chemicals that damaged Flint's old lead water pipes. Brown water flowed into Flint homes. Residents had rashes and eye problems, and their hair was falling out. But the government was ignoring the problem.

Lead in drinking water is poisonous. It causes brain damage, especially in children. Hanna-Attisha examined her young patients' medical records. She announced shocking data at a hospital news conference. The number of Flint's children with lead poisoning had doubled since residents began drinking Flint River's water. Flint residents and activists sued the government. A judge ordered city officials to provide bottled water. The government was also required to replace the lead pipes.

Hanna-Attisha helped establish the Flint Child Health & Development Fund. It has collected millions of dollars in donations. That money provides Flint's children with medical care, play spaces, and more.

CHAPTER FOUR

CONNECTING CULTURES

Having been influenced by diverse cultures and experiences, immigrants to the U.S. often bring new ideas. They offer new ways of expressing these ideas and have influenced others. They have started movements that change U.S. culture.

JOSEPH PULITZER

(1847–1911)
Born in Makó, Hungary

Here, Joseph Pulitzer's portrait is shown with two of his famous newspapers.

Joseph Pulitzer arrived in the U.S. in 1864. He was a teenager with little money. He joined the Union Army as a soldier in the Civil War (1861–1865). Later, he taught himself English in a St. Louis, Missouri, library. There he met editors from the local newspaper. They hired him as a reporter. By age 25, Pulitzer was in charge of a newspaper. In 1883, he bought *New York World*. Pulitzer changed the way newspapers serve readers.

In the 1800s, wealthy and powerful people funded most newspapers. As a result, their ideas and interests influenced what was printed. Newspaper articles were often dull lists of facts. Pulitzer introduced a new approach. He did not look for wealthy supporters. Instead, he charged readers a small amount for his newspapers.

Pulitzer worked hard to please newspaper customers. He printed a variety of opinions, accurate information, and good stories. Illustrations, photographs, and comics filled the pages. Reporters wrote about working people's lives, sports, and fashion. The newspaper was also a tool for justice. It reported on people who did not pay taxes, businesses that treated customers unfairly, and organized gambling. Pulitzer created annual awards, the first of which were given in 1917. They recognize excellent newspaper writing that serves the public good. Those awards are given out to this day.

MONEY FOR A STATUE

In 1885, the Statue of Liberty was ready to be installed on an island in New York Harbor. But the city could not afford to buy a stone pedestal. It cost more than $6 million in today's currency. Joseph Pulitzer started a fundraising campaign in *New York World*. He asked readers for donations. More than 160,000 people sent money. He published all their names. The donors included businesspeople, politicians, street cleaners, and children. They raised more money than Pulitzer requested.

Joseph Pulitzer started a successful campaign to raise money to build a pedestal for the Statue of Liberty.

CLAUDE McKAY

(1889–1948)
Born in Clarendon, Jamaica

Claude McKay arrived in Alabama in 1912. He was already a published poet. Two years later, he moved north. So did thousands of other Black Americans. They were escaping the South's deep racism. McKay settled in Harlem in New York City. In the 1910s, writers, artists, and musicians began creating works that showed pride in Black culture. It was called the Harlem Renaissance. McKay was one of the earliest writers of this movement. Other famous writers were Langston Hughes and Zora Neale Hurston.

One of McKay's poems hinted at the coming movement. It was published in 1919. "If We Must Die" has a defiant tone. It describes fighting back against injustice. McKay had experienced racism in the U.S. He also experienced it in Jamaica, a country then under British rule. McKay's poem invites everyone to join the struggle against injustice.

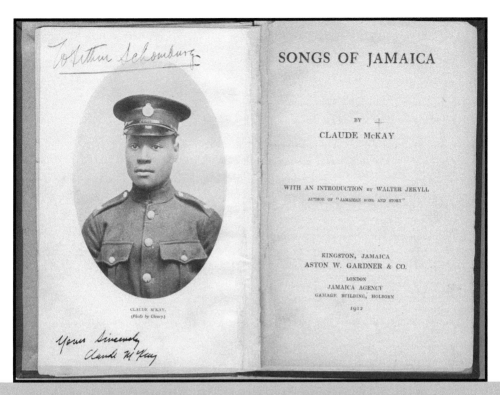

Claude McKay inscribed one of his books to Arthur Schomburg, a Black historian and writer from Puerto Rico who was also active in the Harlem Renaissance.

During the Harlem Renaissance, the works of Black writers finally became widely popular. McKay's 1928 book, *Home to Harlem*, was the first best-selling novel by a Black author. He gave readers a detailed view of the racism and poverty Black people faced in Harlem.

HANYA HOLM

(1893–1992)
Born in Worms, Germany

Hanya Holm arrived in New York City in 1931. Soon, she opened a school. She taught dance in a way that rebelled against ballet's strict rules. Holm pushed students to use their bodies to express emotions in personal ways. She helped invent American modern dance.

Hanya Holm (center) was an innovator in modern dance.

Holm also choreographed dances. This means she planned the movements. She choreographed the first modern dance with prerecorded sound. Between giant columns, 33 dancers performed *Trend* in 1937. It received the *New York Times* Award for Best Dance.

Holm made TV history in 1939. This was the year TV was introduced at the World's Fair in New York City. Holm performed a dance called *Metropolitan Daily* at NBC Studios. People could watch at home if they had TV sets. But TV signals reached only 50 miles (80 km) from New York City. This was the first live telecast of a modern dance.

Holm wanted dancers to have the power to protect their ideas. Copyright laws allow people to own unique ideas as property. In 1952, Holm was the first person to copyright a dance. Holm used a written code developed in the 1920s to record human movement. It was choreography for the musical *Kiss Me, Kate.*

(1904–1997)
Born in Rotterdam, the Netherlands

Willem de Kooning studied painting in art school. He dreamed of traveling to the U.S. In 1926, at age 22, de Kooning hid on a ship and headed to New York City. Many artists were already there. They shared ideas at cafés and in art studios. By the 1950s, New York City was the center of trendy new art styles. But de Kooning became a famous artist by following his own path.

De Kooning painted in the popular style of abstract expressionists. Their paintings did not display realistic scenes from the world. Instead, they expressed emotions through experiments with paint. Their paintings often display energetic brushstrokes and paint drips.

De Kooning carefully developed his own style. For example, he spent almost two years on the painting he called *Woman 1*. He completed it in 1953.

Woman 1, *Woman 2*, and *Woman as Landscape* on display in a museum in London, England

Human figures often appear in de Kooning's paintings. Some people thought these figures made his paintings old-fashioned. Others found them frightening. De Kooning did not feel insulted. He never stopped painting in his own independent way. Today de Kooning is considered a great master of 20th century art.

(1942–)
Born in Lima, Peru

Isabel Allende became a writer after leaving her home as a refugee. In 1973, her family fled Chile after a military dictator took over. From Venezuela, she wrote a letter to her grandfather. It inspired her first novel, *The House of the Spirits*. It was published in 1982 and became a best-seller. Since then, she has written 23 books. Allende moved to California in the 1980s and learned English. She is likely the most widely read Spanish-language author in the world. Allende's books have been translated into 35 languages. They have sold more than 70 million copies.

Allende's unique storytelling style blends facts and fantasy. Allende's characters often face loneliness and challenges. As a refugee, Allende did too. In *Daughter of Fortune*, Allende wrote the fictional story of a Chilean woman. She moves to California to search for gold. In *Ines of My Soul*, Allende also wrote a fictional story. But she was inspired by a real female Spanish

Isabel Allende fled Chile when it became a military dictatorship. When it returned to democracy, she met with the president of Chile at a White House dinner in 1997.

explorer. Allende often adds magical elements to her fiction, such as characters who can read minds. Allende wrote about her daughter's battle against a grave illness in the nonfiction book *Paula*.

The National Book Foundation awarded Allende its 2018 Medal for Distinguished Contribution to American Letters. It honors her important role in Latin American literature.

YO-YO MA

(1955–)
Born in Paris, France

Yo-Yo Ma has played the cello since he was a child. He now uses his cello to help unite people worldwide.

Seven-year-old Yo-Yo Ma was invited to study in New York City in 1962. That year, Ma became a student at the Julliard School of Music. He became a world-famous cellist. Ma uses music to bring cultures together. He speaks both French and Mandarin Chinese. His parents were born in China, then moved to France. For decades, Ma has traveled around the world. He has helped composers, performers, and audiences connect.

Ma often mixes instruments from different cultures. These performances are like conversations in many languages. In the late 1990s, Ma launched the Silk Road Project. The name was inspired by the path traders followed until the 1400s. It stretched between the Mediterranean Sea and Japan. Project musicians play Western instruments like a violin. Or they may play Eastern instruments like a Japanese flute called a *shakuhachi*. Audiences hear these unique combinations at outdoor festivals, concert halls, and school classrooms.

Ma also uses well-known music to connect people. German composer Johann Sebastian Bach's famous music is 300 years old. Starting in 2018, Ma has performed Bach in worldwide locations. He believes this music is a language anyone can understand.

MUSIC WITH A MESSAGE

Yo-Yo Ma is an activist who uses his cello to send a message. He performed near the Juarez-Lincoln International Bridge in Laredo, Texas, on April 13, 2019. This location is along the border between the U.S. and Mexico. He chose this location to bring attention to the challenges immigrants face there. It also celebrates a place where cultures mix.

In 2019, Yo-Yo Ma performed on the U.S.-Mexican border to highlight what united U.S. and Mexican cultures.

1873 Levi Strauss and Jacob Davis receive a patent for work pants with rivets that become known as "jeans."

1883 Joseph Pulitzer buys *New York World* and turns it into one of the most influential newspapers in the nation.

1891 James Naismith invents the game of basketball.

1893 Millions of visitors to the Chicago World's Fair see 100,000 electric lamps powered by Nikola Tesla's new alternating current motor design.

1915 Albert Einstein introduces the general theory of relativity, which changes the world of physics.

1928 Claude McKay publishes *Home to Harlem*, the first best-selling novel by a Black writer.

1939 Giuliana Tesoro moves to the U.S. to complete her training as a chemist and begins her career developing flame-retardant fibers.

1942 Hedy Lamarr and collaborator George Antheil patent a "Secret Communications System" that sends complex messages on changing frequencies.

1952 Hanya Holm receives the first copyright for a dance.

1953 Willem de Kooning completes *Woman 1*. It is the first in a series of paintings that earn him international fame.

1969 Elisabeth Kübler-Ross publishes *On Death and Dying*, which describes her findings on the five stages of grief.

1972 The first home video gaming system, the Magnavox Odyssey, designed by Ralph Baer, is available for sale.

1972 Fazlur Rahman Khan's structural design for New York City's World Trade Center helps it capture the title of the world's tallest building.

1973 Mario Molina discovers that CFCs damage Earth's ozone layer.

1976 Nadia Comaneci stuns the world with seven perfect scores at the 1976 Olympics in Montreal, Canada.

1982 Isabel Allende publishes *House of the Spirits* and gains international fame.

1983 Subrahmanyan Chandrasekhar wins the Nobel Prize in Physics for calculating how dying stars can collapse into black holes.

1986 Liz Claiborne's company makes *Fortune* magazine's list of the most successful businesses in the U.S., becoming the first one on this list led by a female chief executive officer.

Rita Levi-Montalcini and Stanley Cohen share the 1986 Nobel Prize in Medicine for discovering a protein that has helped with research into many diseases.

1996 Madeleine Albright becomes the first female secretary of state of the United States.

David Ho develops antiretroviral therapy treatment (ART) that allows HIV/AIDS patients to live longer, healthier lives.

1997 Sergey Brin and Larry Page register the Google domain.

2003 Elon Musk founds electric car company Tesla Motors.

2015 Mona Hanna-Attisha discovers that Flint, Michigan's, drinking water has given thousands of children lead poisoning.

2018 Yo-Yo Ma launches the Silk Road Project to encourage understanding and acceptance between cultures.

GLOSSARY

activist (AK-tuh-vist)—a person who works for social or political change

asylum (uh-SAHY-luhm)—a place of retreat and safety from danger

council (KOUN-suhl)—an official group that consults with or advises a government

entrepreneur (ahn-truh-pruh-NUR)—a person who creates and runs a business

fascist (FA-shist)—having to do with a form of government run by a dictator that promotes extreme nationalism and racial prejudice

Nazi (NOT-see)—having to do with a political party that controlled Germany from 1933 to 1945, led by Adolf Hitler and responsible for the murder of about 6 million Jewish people and others

patented (PAT-uhnt-ed)—legally protected against being used, copied, or sold by someone other than the owner

physics (FIZ-iks)—a form of science that deals with energy and matter in space and time

prejudice (PREJ-uh-diss)—a negative opinion of something or someone not based in fact or experience

refugee (ref-yuh-JEE)—a person who leaves a home country because he or she is in danger

READ MORE

Grimes, Nikki. *One Last Word: Wisdom from the Harlem Renaissance.* New York: Bloomsbury, 2017.

Peters, Stephanie True. *Groundbreaking Guys: 40 Men Who Became Great by Doing Good.* New York: Little, Brown and Company, 2019.

Vecchione, Patrice. *Ink Knows No Borders: Poems of the Immigrant and Refugee Experience.* New York: Triangle Square, 2019.

Wallace, Sandra Neil. *First Generation: 36 Trailblazing Immigrants and Refugees Who Make America Great.* New York: Little, Brown Books for Young Readers, 2018.

INTERNET SITES

Construction, History of Skyscrapers, and More
www.pbs.org/wgbh/buildingbig/skyscraper/basics.html

Flint Water Crisis Activism
www.maricopeny.com/about

Harlem Renaissance
www.brainpop.com/games/timezonexharlemrenaissance

Nikola Tesla's Life and Innovation
tesla.aziznatour.com

INDEX